SIDEBROW BOOKS

SISTER URN

Published by Sidebrow Books
P.O. Box 86921
Portland, OR 97286
sidebrow@sidebrow.net
www.sidebrow.net

Cover art by Josie Morway
Cover & book design by Jason Snyder

ISBN: 1-940090-09-1
ISBN-13: 978-1-940090-09-2

FIRST EDITION | FIRST PRINTING
9 8 7 6 5 4 3 2 1
SIDEBROW BOOKS 020
PRINTED IN THE UNITED STATES

Sidebrow Books titles are distributed by
Small Press Distribution

Titles are available directly from Sidebrow at
www.sidebrow.net/books

A Member of

www.theintersection.org

Sidebrow is a member of the Intersection Incubator, a program of
Intersection for the Arts (www.theintersection.org) providing fiscal
sponsorship, incubation, and consulting for artists. Contributions
to Sidebrow are tax-deductible to the extent allowed by law.

SISTER URN

ANDREA REXILIUS

SIDEBROW BOOKS • 2019 • PORTLAND & SAN FRANCISCO

for my sister, Andrea Erki (4/30/1979 - 5/3/2017)

SISTER URN

We were quite different, but we belonged together, we were more than the sum of our two selves, we were allies, we made our own community, and that is rare in life.

— Sándor Márai, *Embers*

Andrea and I flocked together. Andrea and I played jump rope and tetherball at recess. Andrea and I got our periods. I showed Andrea how to insert a tampon. I showed Andrea how to take a shower with me instead of with her mother. Andrea and I played by the Fox River digging up fake clamshells and drowning Barbie dolls. Andrea and I walked down the railroad tracks to the sewage plant and climbed on a hill of shit that felt like muddy Jell-O. Andrea and I played with her mother's Hungarian tarot cards. I bit Andrea on the back of the neck and left behind teeth marks. I dropped Andrea and she hit her head on the radiator and grew a tiny blue egg on the middle of her forehead. Andrea and I rode a yellow bicycle built for two. Andrea was a stunt double. She always flew over the handlebars, flipped in the air, and rolled to a stop. The other Andrea was less stunt-like. She would land underneath the bike, scraped by the sidewalk and the bicycle chain. Andrea left moldy glasses of milk in our bedroom. Andrea listened to Prince and Madonna. Andrea didn't like that her mother had an accent and didn't shave her armpits. The other Andrea stayed in her room reading books. The other Andrea began huffing glue. The other Andrea almost had sex at a seventh grade orgy until Ramon Santiago's mother stormed in. Andrea and Andrea both snuck out of the house when Andrea's father shoved them into the walls. Andrea and Andrea set the kitchen floor on fire. Andrea and Andrea would spray their hands with hairspray and set their hands on fire. The two Andreas scared away all the boys with their twin powers and spooky Hungarian music. Andrea and Andrea practiced witchcraft. One Andrea wrote down the name of the boy she liked, rolled up the paper, tied it with string, and submerged it in a jar of water. Andrea dated a boy who made graffiti art. The other Andrea dated a boy who wore women's clothing. Andrea became homecoming queen. Andrea began getting Fs in school. Andrea pierced her ears with a hot needle. Andrea began smoking cigarettes. Andrea cut her hair, long on one side, falling over her eyes, and short on the other. Andrea was a cheerleader. Andrea was suspended for selling drugs. She gave a boy a pill that made his pee turn blue. He vomited blue bile all over science class. The other Andrea went to raves. Andrea began taking acid and ecstasy. Andrea is bisexual. Andrea was good at math and drawing. The other Andrea preferred English class and performance art. The first Andrea and the second Andrea pulled stockings over their faces so they would look like androgynous muggers. When the first Andrea's father choked the second Andrea, the first Andrea kicked her father in the chest until he let go. Andrea became addicted to heroin. Andrea moved away. The Andreas reunited in high school playing badminton in P.E. class. "This is my sister, Andrea," Andrea would say to her friends, who would get upset by this duplication of Andreas. A boy claimed to have made out with one of the Andreas at a party, but he called the wrong Andrea to follow up. One of the Andreas loved a boy until he loved Ayn Rand and she decided not to love him anymore. One Andrea became a stripper because she liked to dance and the money was good. The first Andrea shoved rum balls down the second Andrea's throat to get her drunk. Both Andreas would pee out of the second story window of their room at night. One Andrea jumped off the roof. The other Andrea was too scared and went out the bathroom window. Andrea developed ulcers. Andrea tried to die. Early on, both of the Andreas stayed home sick and watched *License to Drive* and *The Lost Boys*. This is how one of the Andreas learned to speak English. How could a billion Chinese people be wrong, Andrea? Both of the Andreas were sexually assaulted. One of them was raped. Andrea enjoys watching *Law and Order: SVU*. So does the other Andrea. Dun. Dun. Andrea's mother said blue-eyed people are not to be trusted, even though she has blue eyes herself. Andrea is addicted to prescription drugs and has severe anxiety. Both of the Andreas have brown eyes. The Andreas do not look alike. The Andreas are not related by blood. Both Andreas prefer orange cats because those are the color cats they grew up with. It is rare when the Andreas talk to each other now. The Andreas like to get high together and watch thrillers on TV. They give each other pedicures and do face masks and talk about the past. If you put two Andreas in a room together, they will speak from the shock of static. Neither of the Andreas will cry about being an Andrea. If you cross an Andrea they will squint their dark brown eyes at you until it feels like you are being punched in the face.

GRAVE

My sister kept in a padlocked box the following items:

1. A photo of her parents on their wedding day.
2. Hungarian coins & bills.
3. A ponytail of her hair, tied with a blue ribbon.
4. Burlesque matchboxes.
5. Letters from her ex-girlfriend, Callie. The same girlfriend who got her hooked on heroin when she was 19 years old.
6. Middle school photos of herself as a cheerleader.
7. A purple pouch full of polished stones.
8. The deck of Hungarian tarot cards we played with when we were young.
9. Thirty-eight pictures of kittens.

GRAVITY

This is the line of outcome.

Gravity of a vein's collapse
or a heart giving way
paper thin, already
made of ash.

Afterwards we gathered you
into pails or buckets,
into plastic bags tied shut
with string.

Skyward and across
the Atlantic.

I went to a place without trees
to sever your mind from mine.

You were always so hungry,
or cold. Nearly a ghost.

Still, everyone will say
what was it like to lose a sister.

What was it like to see her body
embalmed within church walls
in your hometown.

GRIEF

Who cross into orphanages of air
find flight. The flightless
carve spaces, remove need.
Ghost the expanse.
Walls, windows
into the next.

Some say a thick black line.
Drawn taut against the curvature,
an etching into
cut open round bowl,
a god's home. Meridian.

Beneath the roots
of a fallen tree. See.

A / HEM

Stitch is hermeneutical method.
An architecture,
or how a nest /
constructed by scavenging.
Sister. / Bestiary's arrival.
Our blood oath /
building toward heat of the egg.
Paradox is not how another's body
frames your own body.
Her scripture /
flesh of my flesh,
blood of my blood. / A hem.
Relationship between consummate,
consumption, and consume.

SISTER / HYMN

Grief returns as graceful turn toward horizon line.

Oh, sister. *Mindig szeretni foglak.* Serene fog rises in my mind. Thinking of her in water. Covered in rain. Cloud swirling at the center of her. Tongue a possessed hurricane. I don't believe in demons. Though she always dreamt of them. Woke drenched and thunderous. *Csúszik a jegyzetek az összes ereszbe.* My only sister. My predator. My prey.

Pray sister, for the light in your eyes to lift. Pray for better weather. *Magyarul imádkozz.* It is too late for my sister, who wore a crown of thorns. The hunter inside her ate her vocal chords.

Her breath rose as mist in May 3rd rain. *A legbátrabb húgom/nővér.* Beware. A novel is a bear trap. Dear sister, your legs.

SELF-EDGE

In a poem, one Andrea may hide another Andrea.

SELVEDGE

If I could tell you what I need to say, I would tell you fission, entropy, a hallway.
Translate this into what is elemental.
I would be carbon.

You can photograph me.
You can trace me onto your wall and leave a shadow where my breath fell
when you did not hear what I was saying. I said, I would be carbon.

Don't choke on the back of my neck. It is small. Swallow it.
Lose it in glass bathrooms where it blends in
with crystal chandeliers and tile shaped like ribbons.

You are agnostic.
But I love you. Hydrogen. Hydrogen. Hydrogen.
When you go I'll be frightened. When you go I reconstitute.

DEAR ANDREA [I SPEAK IN TONGUES]

First Letter: Súly

Sister, the selvedge is a location and a pressure. Almost a seam, raw in its potential untwining. You are a snow globe; a bright red mutable desire. The city wept for days to put out your flames. Dear Tsunami, Dear Egress. A dress is a shape for housing you. Address is inescapable concern. To be seen. To be envisioned. Sister, I saw your fame in the empty envelopes you never sent. I saw your self-edge. Saw your blood-stained war you wore, unravel.

Kedves húgom, a varrás egyfajta nyomás. Egy szakadatlan fészek. Te egy hófehér, egy élénk vörös változékony vágy vagy. A város napokig sírt, hogy tegye ki a lángjait. Kedves Tsunami, Kedves Egress. A ruha olyan formájú, hogy otthont nyújtson. A cím elkerülhetetlen aggodalomra ad okot. Látható. Elképzelni. Húgom, láttam a hírneved az üres borítékban, amit soha nem küldtél el. Láttam a te saját széleidet. Láttad azokat a háborúkat, amiket felderítettél.

Dear Sister, this seed place provides pressure. It is almost sewing but raw in its potential wreck. You are snow white, a lively red lustful desire. The city cried for days to put out its flames. Dear Tsunami, Dear Egress. The dress is in a shape to provide a home for you. This title is of inevitable concern. Visible. Imagine sister. I saw the fame in the empty envelope I never sent. I saw your edges. You saw the wars you explored.

Second Letter: Gyász

Below is a symbol of scripture, yet none will confess hope. You like the beast. Its membrane of isms. Our paradox is not how the other body becomes its own body. That part is obvious, flesh of my skin, blood of my organ. Like the relationship between consumption, posthumous consumption.

Öltés / hermeneutikai módszer.
Építészet, vagy ahogy ásod a fészket.
Húgom, sztori lesz érkezés.
Vér eskü / újjászületés.
Paradox / nem az, hogy a másik teste a saját testét keresi.
Szentírásom testem húsának, vérem vérének. A szívem a lelkem szíve.
Elégedett a szíved és az újjáéledésed

Stitch / hermeneutical method. Architecture, or as you dig a nest / building it. Sister / bestiary will be arrival. Blood oath / building toward the egg's heat. The heat of the page. Paradoxical / is not that the other body is looking for its own body. My Sacred Scripture / Our Body, not the blood of my blood. / One hem. The relationship between postulate, posture, and composure.

Third Letter: Kegyelem

Szeretnék beszélni veled a szívédel. Azt akarom mondani, hogy sajnálom, hogy a szálak nem kötődtek. Még mindig úgy érzem, hogy hozzám kötődtél. Még mindig a nevemben tartom a neved. Még mindig tartsd meg, hogy ki vagy és ki vagyok én. Mi látjuk ugyanaszt a színt. És ugyanazokat a bánatos sebeket énekeljük. Hallgatom az égbolt dalát. Madár lettél. Amikor az eső esik, tudom, hogy megérkezett.

I want to talk to you in her heart. To say I'm sorry the threads are not tied. I still feel bound to me. I still keep your name in my name. Hold who you are, who I am. We see the same color. And we sing the same wicked wounds. Listen to the song of the sky. You're the bird. When rain falls, I know it's here.

Final Letter: Spirit of the Calling

If I could understand what to say, I would betray the cleavage, the trophy, the corridor. Translate this item. I would be charcoal. You can shoot. You can go to the wall and leave a shadow where my breath has fallen. When you did not hear what I said. I said I would be charcoal. Do not shy away from my back. It's small. Swallow it. Be in the glass bathroom where it melts with crystal chandeliers and tile-shaped ribbons. You're agnostic. But I love you. Hydrogen. Hydrogen. Hydrogen. If you go, I'm scared. When you leave, I constrict.

DEAR SISTER

Here is a nest to fashion a place for yourself in the wider world.

Here's a nettle branch.

An armory.

A mother-scream enclosed.

Memory moves away from poems.

As weather shifts, something else beckons.

My stuck swallows stitch beaks to the page.

A bright red cardinal crows.

This blank is a bed.

This surface, a deep current of white.

Curve away from the shadow you left.

Draw back.

The cardinal's right.

Go toward sunlight or go toward sunrise.

AXIS / HEM

And then my frame spoke,
and gelding in the throat spoke.
The wheel that turns my hand turns
the earth. I am plant form.
What is an animal?
It does not turn. Its breath
the same as my breath.
It does not turn? A laden cart in throat.
Whose root is less visible. Hooves. Wheels.

RESERVOIR

Your mother told me you suffered from night terrors and that's one of the reasons you took so many pills, an entire bottle in a week. Followed by withdrawal (seizures, nausea, anxiety, insomnia, agoraphobia). I told her she was enabling you. She said she wouldn't put you out on the street. Her mother and father long dead. Her brothers somewhere in Hungary. I saw how the math stacked against you. Did you know you were dying? I stopped visiting after the Christmas you were strung out and set your sweater on fire reaching across a candle. You called your doctor a drug dealer. You'd pay a few hundred and he'd ask if you wanted pills. Yes. And he'd give them to you. Despite the heart palpitations. Despite your arms. Despite your face. Your boyfriend thought you were possessed by a demon. After you died, he wouldn't leave your mother's house. She called the police to have him removed. Your night terrors entered her and I was afraid they would enter me too. In her dream she is naked, chasing you down a narrow street in Budapest, trying to grab your hand before you disappear around a corner with a man in a dark cloak. The night she found you, you were hunched over in the sink. Your face pressed to the mirror. She could see you were no longer breathing.

LÁNYTESTVÉR CISTERN

What one sister dreams of is her other sister.

Salt water cried into her cistern.

What do you remember that I remember of you?

We indicates a place of arrival.

I do not like that phrase, abandoning it dearly.

I do not like leaving.

In our dream, two rivers converge,

then split across the center.

Take the garden.

We blossom as tulips. Dig broken bottles into our palms.

Hopefully there are words inside the bottles.

I was weeping at first, but I wanted to shout too.

I saw *the ghost of the azaleas*, all her guttural glory.

A father in Budapest unraveling, singing out

my sister's nervous winter.

Then she said she wanted to dance with us.

Dear sister. Dear ghost.

UNSTITCH

I sew my tongue to my sister's tongue so we can speak as one Andrea.

I sew my hem to my sister's hem so we become each other's homeland.

I knit my speech to my sister's speech so we can comb our meridian.

I unstitch my shock from my sister's shock and we convulse more violently.

I detach my death from my sister's death so we do not become the same buried body.

I remove my soul from my sister's soil so our body is not entwined silt.

I release my breath from my sister's breath so our agony is not the same enemy.

I relinquish my name from my sister's name so we are no longer Andrea, Andika.

SISTER URN

Dear Andika, your sky has fallen on mud.

Your death-face a broken bolt of lightning.

If there were photographs of the inside of your mouth.

Reverberation caught in a thin stream of white.

Each stroke a time frame. When you zoom out, a horizon.

When you look at blue you realize it's black, variant light seeping.

The direction of any map as its climate.

I'm the unmoored space beneath what you've weathered.

You're the beautiful crumpled terrain, *lánytestvér*.

NESTS OF MAMMALS

Bodies can catch feelings as easily as catch fire: affect leaps from one body to another, evoking tenderness, inciting shame, igniting rage, exciting fear…

— Melissa Gregg, *The Affect Theory Reader*

But if we want to understand feeling, we had better understand all the things that are conjoined and that have evolved to be conjoined. We can tease them apart, we can factor them, we can centrifuge them, but they remain a unitary phenomenon, which exhibits many diverse characteristics at once. Now that is not fashionable in science. It is called contamination. Unfortunately, we are deeply contaminated creatures.

— Silvan S. Tomkins, *Exploring Affect: The Selected Writings of Silvan S. Tomkins*

I went to the savanna to rupture my color, excavating blueprints for our future. The tableau is the former life of the seventeenth century. An image

cast by means of a child in front of a clock. Traces from wound to the coast. Say, I, too, am the afterlife. Here the aftermath is theoretical and therefore

difficult to pin down in objects, and therefore unnamable. The exact opposite of poetry. Which is why poets must fight for clarity. The fog of disillusion

and despair readily swallows all its victims whole. No one wants to be a stuck pig or grabbed by the pussy. This body is not your body. This body is not your

country. The blood I shed from between my legs is a tempest. And that blood is mine to bury or drown or grow into a beautiful rhododendron if that is my

present desire. All my present desires are to escape a wicked contagion. But thank you for the funeral, says Bataille, the savagery that is there. Meanwhile

Roland Barthes analyzes a tiny point of light he takes to be a star but is in fact the glowing tip of a cigarette. Voyeur, he says. Not viewer. Voyeur.

A shadow of a bird cast onto garments of the Statue of Liberty. Wings beating up and down from within. In forensic photographs of Chicago

(my hometown), a womb is edited or inscribed with the art of caves (our hometown). An encounter with present history. Interpreted by Freud as early

collages of white space. Site of water, depression, violence. Our private phantom, attached to our person. Erotic currents of the dream surface in

the emergence of white light. A sense of being suspended, in this fabulous stillness, weightless. Happy that Picasso isn't here for once.

It might emerge as fieldwork ghosts. Memory as research method. I am speaking of a womb as if it were a page. It might emerge as narrative and

what if after all these years it was not wrong to be a woman, and it was not wrong to be a gay man. Only wounds still carry the thrust of their dichotomy:

Depress, make despondent, (fag) weigh down, weigh heavily on, (bitch) cast down, dampen someone's spirits, (pussy) dispirit, dishearten, (cunt) bring

down; deject. Example: "The darkness of the demagogue depressed them."

It is the season of warmth, colorful lights line the houses. Words hearth and mirth arise. But now a weight grows heavily on our chest, like pneumonia.

Lungs unraveling. Therefore language unraveling. I go for walks in the neighborhood and gather loose threads from the city's unhappy bodies. I find

violet threads strung into the nests of birds. Long red threads with the texture of yarn. Short, fine, yellow threads, barely visible. I store these threads of

collective bodies in wooden jewelry boxes which contain many compartments. All of the yellow thoughts, all of the blue intertwining. All a small lake.

On the weekends Eric and I walk to the Museum of Nature and Science to look at taxidermy flamingos, bears, a white albatross, in their semi-natural,

semi-urban habitats. Decorated by molted feathers, grasslands, butterfly wings, one can imagine oneself within the dreamscape of the deer, horror

of being a small fox ripped open by a bear, movement of hind legs, flight of antelope. The longer I stare into the glass cage of nature, the more details

unfold. A nest in a tree. A small frog hidden beneath a thicket of grasses. I want to write poems that are maps of dioramas, with the powerful gash of

sight, like the volta in a sonnet. I look into the eyes of the furthest coyote. Notice a bird in a tree. Find one blue thread tucked, skyward, inside a nest.

Tug at my piece of found thread.

Today we watch nature videos at the Museum of Nature and Science IMAX. A 21st century version of the stereoscope. Our left eyes and our right

eyes come into focus, allowing parallel lines to collapse into one sight, our third eye. In the high-tech 1920s, Eric becomes Max Ernst and I become

Mina Loy. We exit reality to roam with tigers in the projected landscape. We see their textures and peer directly into animal consciousness with our 3D

goggles. Helena Bonham Carter narrates the film. We forget who was elected president. We fall back in love with each other and the world. I want to

remember this discovery when my lungs cave in. What we glimpse in the face of calamity. The distorted syntax of light waves. Our heart softens and opens.

It is a far cry from the sea.

At night instead of sleeping, we watch Bob Ross paint landscapes. Small cabins overlooking cliffs. Alone in the woods, Bob Ross imagines a past life.

It may have been the 1980s. I was two and eight and eleven and then the '90s arrived like a television-style documentary on hip-hop. There is no freedom,

no air to breathe. The last word in the book is "us." The last sentence in the story, "Now go back to sleep."

I am inscribing an invisible sentence on my body. It blooms and retreats like a flower, depending on my mood. On the horizon the soundtrack to

Tarkovsky's *Stalker* is playing. The year is 2016. Many people have died. Many of the people were not famous. I saw M. NourbeSe Philip in a white

dress lighting one hundred white candles. A brightness reaching out, until all our souls pollinate. I will miss her dance in the silent future. But today,

thank god, we are heard.

Eric and I look at dioramas of deer at the museum. We do this every week. We see the Earth from space and learn about the scarcity of water. At home

we listen to Brian Eno and dance like the birds in *The Life of Birds*. On the news the cosmos remembers Sappho's poetry. What has been torn and burnt,

small scraps from our hands will be found again. We have an urge to obtain a metal detector. To feel the sound it makes. To become a Morse code

for ghosts. A sound similar to being found in the trenches. Down below the beeping. I find St. Theresa's lost necklace near the back steps of St. Augustine's

church, now turned cultural center where my friends paint, inspired by a hidden gramophone in a secret room locked away at the center of the

church. The last word in the essay is "time." The first line of the book is, "The poetry of Wallace Stevens makes me happy."

Despite what has been wiped clean, all the erasures of grand sexualites and intellects, the progress we have made as a species, we are still living and we

will fight against a brood that craves our collective extinction. The trees allow us to write our poems on them. They help by steeling us toward great

darknesses to come.

There are stories about the things humans store in trees. I found a human heart, spirit of a sleeping girl, journal of a dying witch, *Amen*. This is the

story of our other life. Eric is an herbalist and I am a bird. I kneel down in front of a book and weep. It is brown and thin, like the Fox River. It tells a

story of women burnt to the ground. Smart, independent women who read books, who study plants, who give birth, who understand phases of the

moon and know the ocean's relationship to blood. The world is not flat in their notebooks. Their wisdom a form of casting flies. Even as a young girl,

I knew these women. I felt I was one of them.

In the book's prior life, it is a lake preserved in ice. The verb *lake* is first recorded in 1922. The first action is the beak of a small bird holding a piece

of thread. Inside the thread the following items: soil, a mirror, a sentence. The sun is born so we can view the blank page. Its ripples, curves, undercurrents.

Its deluge. The word *deluge* is also a mating dance. The bird reveals his text to his lady. An egg is born. And from the egg, a world. Beneath the surface

of the poem, a bird unravels subtexts and contexts, or textures of threads until a narrative rises to the mouth of the lake. As the wind rises, sounds of

childhood return. The bird soars over a vast forest of pine trees. It sounds like pages being torn from a book. But the song the child sings has no

rhetoric. *Trees don't need your rhetoric*, I tell her. A bird searches, carving out entrails in the light. Disparate images gather in the beak of the bird, become

a bramble for birthing exposure. This is how listening cures the air. The breath of the bird in the sky humming. Her flight lines create a map of

memory. How we have traveled before. Echo of a past life, or a blueprint. Life lines buried in the architecture of a tree, or a body.

For example, patterns are a wolf, or a vocabulary. In the past tense of the text I am on the hunt for an estuary. Investigating caverns of phonemes.

I find Gertrude Stein along the way. Gertrude listens to the repetitive skip of the bird's wings. Dear Gertrude, I say, reading a phoneme is like reading

braille. Use your senses. Follow the metal in your blood. Become a brood. A sentence. Become a tone of certainty. At the center of the book there is a

premonition. It is one grounded in etymology.

By the bank of the river I lost my voice I lost my vocal chords in the water at the bank of the dank, dark river I lost my speech in the wetness my virginity

eroded at the bank of my under self. I lost my senses when I drank I lost a river within me roots may be taken out of the river I lost my name I lost the

nape of my neck it was not glorious it was a woman planted three inches deep in a well the water was full of blood. The well was full of blood my

father said *drink, drink*. When the stalks are decayed, when the well is buried, when the ground swells, when the seed decays, when the thread dries, we will

remove a river from your mouth. This river's story is childhood. Another river is the story of rape. The polluted river is the one I drown inside of, the one

I wrote letters to, sinking words down into the bottomless dark. In this descent we pay attention to language, to shifting patterns of weather. The nuances

of how we relate to one another. It is called being silent listening, feeling the undercurrents of movement, how the line tugs on our collectivity.

Ethics shouldn't be about control, but passion for possibility. Most times I notice it is mainly about the ways in which we pollinate, what we do in

consent, with our genitals. I am a cellular organism, a small garden of life. While others attempt to construct walls around me, I find ways to reach the

sun. You cannot control the way a flower blooms. But now the catastrophe has turned literal. Poisoning the soil, taxing the water, bulldozing people off

of the land. Soon the sky will be off limits. Brooks will be burned. The poets strung up like witches. The scientists atomized. And.

This is the vision of the fatherland. But an ethics should not be built from suffering. It is an act of Eros. Beauty. The father doesn't understand this, but

it is why I will always turn the salt he pours on our wound into a stark blue ravishing sea. I'm not sorry. I won't meet you in the afterlife. I believe in

molecules and movement. Transference of energy from one plain to the next. I find the field you are tilling to be disgusting. But don't fret, when you

weren't looking, I hid the heart of a hawk. Deep down in death, a spark of involution.

Today we go to a living museum, look into faces of tigers, keep console with red pandas, cry when coyotes pace. It is an act of preservation. To dream

the hatch is lifted. To feel unencumbered air and hear wonder inside our constitutional growling. The ghost of Emily Dickinson laps at my ear, her

voice a howling wind of dashed variance. Years ago I saw Emily perched at the top of a pine tree in Northern California. She took the form of an

albatross. As I stared, my bike veered into oncoming traffic. Dear Emily, you are a prayer for death. In the sun's future life it is a monsoon. The phrase on

the tip of its tongue is a jet wave. We are waiting for the world to end. For the light to retreat into the dark vast insurmountable landscape without land.

In this endless geography the birds carve out lines into the white space. The birds huddle into larger masses. As spheres bursting with color. With so

much mitigation, the birds grow tired.

In the beginning there was an emotion. A shifting of tectonic plates inside the collective body. Bright red streaks of light. A pupil dilating. The death

of a swan. We are waiting for the world to end. We are waiting for soot to rise and all the birds to return to earth. Where light will fluctuate into a new

story. The breath of each animal sutured against the dark sky. Why is the sky blue, a child asks. Because it is alive and made of moisture. Ten percent of a

bird's body mass is water. Goldfinches, cactus wrens, curve-billed thrashers are all dying. Meanwhile the heat is wild. And flying to other habitats a

slow and womanly migration. A man does not ask for directions to another planet. He'd rather die ruining and rigging the current one. Because the

unconscious is impregnable. Arriving over and over. The repetition of men accumulates. You can hold them for a time. Most of all don't go into the

forest. Men have committed the greatest crimes against women there. He has spoiled her beehives, her ocean, the moon. Sought out his own monthly

bloodshed by slaughtering his motherland. The songbird, the thrush, the meadowland. The lark.

Today the man is painting a cabin in the woods to represent his loneliness. To come to the blank page after success in war; his desire for representational

beauty. He says he became the host of his own television painting show for his mother. Perhaps so she might recognize his softer side, his face when it is

turned away from death. The man creates entire forests with the slightest gesture of his palette knife. A sky clear of any birds. Trees without animals.

Cabins empty of their men. To look upon the possibility of a habitat. That is all the man wants.

And what of women. What do the women want? After war the women paint with the blood inside of them. The story the blood tells is one of

perpetual wanting. It is a story of brutality against the female body and therefore against mankind. A story of hatred and humiliation. The man's

story of control. But when the woman's blood writes, it is something else. A deep, animal scream, from the bowels of cremation. For the woman is

already her own habitat. She is a tree, and a nest, and her body births the bird. And by bird, I mean language. It is why humans are obsessed with

caverns, with concaves, with the hollow of a woman's throat. We are waiting for the egg to hatch. We are waiting for a sentence to be found. For a

narrative to lift her dress and show us the ravine. A sentence is not a road, or a watermark, Walt Whitman. A sentence is a slit throat. A woman's throat

waiting for the bird to return.

We are waiting for the sentence to find its new nest. A logic beneath the tangled stitch of embroidery. What is caught behind the image. If you study

the threads long enough you will see the nest as a living organism. An origami of sorts. The hand folding a piece of paper into a world the paper

crane rests upon. A thread, like a paint stroke creates an image and inside each image is a nexus. The way a nucleus forms around a central emotion.

When the body is massaged, the body sentences. Each atom a point of light, an energy, an alphabet eclipsed.

I am writing this essay one thread at a time, as the days move me. At times it is too hard to speak. What would I say? Things are difficult. Disturbing.

They always have been. I am more or less safe. The weather is neutral. It hasn't been a bad winter. Except for the tempest stirring.

I'd like to draw a parallel between the disbelief in climate change and what is happening socially. On all levels, a denial of legitimacy. The alternative

facts cannot change the facts. The ice will still melt. The body will still abide by its own tendencies. The erotica of self-knowing will stay godly.

You cannot read into a text, what is not within that text. It will erupt into a glacier dying before you get to the final sentence. Curtain call. The mountains

are bowing. The lakes are bowing. We have already said good-bye to the west african black rhinoceros. The pyrenean ibex has taken her final bow. Throw

your flowers to the passenger pigeon. Bid adieu to the mountain deer, the armadillo, the bison. Say your goodbyes to Prince, Princess Leia, Pauline

Oliveros, David Bowie. The ground sloth, the jaguar, the golden bear, the great domestic housecat, Virginia. Also the antelope, the island vole, the

mexican grizzly bear, the barn owl, the parakeet, the hawk, the heron, the ivory-billed woodpecker, the dusky seaside sparrow, the indigo-capped

hummingbird, the jamaican whippoorwill. But no matter. These are words. A list.

At the Museum of Nature and Science I reinterpret nature's mythologies. *The Story of Beauty and the Beast.* If I were a woman of the plains in my

former life, I would choose a love life with the buffalo. Not wanting to be a vessel or a maid for the men, I would find my love affair, spiritual, emotional,

with this great woolly mammal. We would grow old together and commune beneath the hot sun of the plains. I would weave flowers into the belly of my

buffalo, comb his thick locks. His animal eye opening galaxies for me. I in turn would try not to scar him with the human. At the museum I tell my

tale to Eric. Running my fingers through a swatch of buffalo fur, I whisper in his ear, *The Erotics of the Buffalo.* The following week we decide to visit

the zoo. To look inside the living eyes of animals. I do not find a buffalo. I find a little girl.

In the previous life of the girl, she was a glacier. In *The Small Backs of Children*, Lidia Yuknavitch suggests that a girl is symbolic for a larger destructive

context. Her book asks, among other things, is the way a society treats women/girls indicative of the way that society treats itself, its people and its

landscape? The short answer is yes. Strikingly so. I pull two images off the internet. The Venus of Willendorf and a female cyborg. Now that I am

nearing 40, my body is becoming sculptural. I have decided to embrace it. This is an act of faith, an act of extreme, physical revolt in the face of a

society bent on self-erasure and self-demolition. The Venus of Willendorf harkens back to a time when it was okay for women to take up space. When

their folds, and their sexualities, not just their reproductive capacities, were revered. A woman made of clay. A woman as sultry, seductive fertility goddess.

Fertility meaning all things. The water. The land. The seeds we plant in the earth. In the cyborgian context, female landscape is desolation and war.

In the past life of war, it was a sternum. Or a stern man shaking his fist in the clouds. Dear Freud, the more dangerous thing is womb envy. True strength

is not overpowering. It is protective. A collaboration of cellular forces. And what emerges is not an emergency. In the past life of the fetal matter, it was

the yellow dust of pollen. Beautiful, but something you could rub between your fingers and let go in the wind. A circular process, rather than a linear

one. Dear Men, I do not want you inside my poem, and yet, here you are. Raping girls, putting your proprietary stamp upon other people's ovaries,

and assholes. Who made you the authority? Oh, right. You did. In the image of yourself. The better wisdoms of the father. Going against the grain.

Riding the current in the wrong direction. Controlling the gifts, instead of cultivating them. Stupid men. Whose muscles are a lame intellect. Whose

dicks are a battalion instead of a filament. Calm the fuck down; we just want to be able to love you.

I thought I was writing this poem to prepare for the extinction of the planet. It turns out I was writing this essay to prepare for the death of my cat.

Her passage a clearer species-based emoting. Or as Grace Paley once put it, "There will never be another cat like Virginia." In the afterlife of the cat,

she is a bouquet of flowers. The burning flame of a white votive candle. A hummingbird in the collage of "Fanciful Animals" newly taped to our

refrigerator. In the other lives of the cat, she was my familiar. In the future, I will be her hag again. Symbiosis of species is transcendent. I breathe her

fur into my lungs; she whispers her last breath onto my sternum. Her name was Maya Deren. Her name was Mina Loy. The grey ghost wolf. The grey

specter in the window. In the beginning, Mina Loy hid a grain of pollen in every piece of paper. In the beginning, Maya Deren bought a black suit.

In the beginning, the very beginning, she enjoyed playing with ribbons or yarn.

The last line of the paragraph is, "The horizon glows in the distance." It is bright pink or bright orange with a layer of blue underneath. Bob Ross says

no sky palette would be complete without a deep rust or a flickering ember fresh from the burning ash of the body. I thought I was writing this poem to

prepare for the snuff films of the patriarchy. It turns out I was writing it to prepare for the death of my Hungarian sister.

Now that all of the animals have died, Eric and I go to the aquarium to visit the fish. It's a 1980s dance party of the eye. Sink or swim. Salt heals all

wounds. Is it salt that does that? If I can't go to the ocean, I will simulate it. I dress up as Marie Antoinette. I wear a powder blue pompadour wig and

paint myself porcelain. Flies gather on my arms and face. I hold a statuesque pose as the flies swarm. In my past life in California I became a different

person every day. Alone in a basement with costumes, studying books on fashion in the 1920s, the Victorian Era, the Wild West. I hemmed clothes

and made simple alterations. I played music and took naps on the Santa Claus stomachs when I got bored. At the costume store I dressed up as the

following ladies: 1920s Debutant, Windup Doll, Graveyard-Shift Librarian, Taxidermy Bird, Dolly Parton, Bearded Lady, Accordion-Playing Sailor,

Russian Futurist, Trapeze Artist, Clown. I gave myself the Russian spy name, Visteria Dostcheckovich. Visteria is sultry and mysterious. She wears

beaded gowns and smokes cigarettes from a 1920s cigarette holder. When in disguise, she wears corduroy suits and elaborate mustaches and calls herself,

Anastasia Vawn. Whenever I'm sad or mourning the death of something: a sister, democracy, women's rights, academia. I wish I were in California.

In California you can walk the road for days eating grapefruit, blackberries, and figs from the landscape around you. You can live in a sailboat or a tool

shed in your friend's parent's backyard next to an abandoned peach orchard with a path that leads to the American River. You can sleep on the ground

or in a pine tree. I spent seven years of my life inside a river in Northern California.

The last drop of water is a vowel. The last grain of sand is a morsel. The last bird in the sky is a cartographer. The last cartographer, an explosion.

Falling ash is a murky place to be. One cannot see the road. Is there even a road? One cannot see the sky. Is there still a sky? There are no ideas but in

things, but in our current climate there are no ideas, only things. And all of the doctors are dead. I am willing to excavate the mineral that lurks beneath

the surface of the white page. To plant my words here. Always. And to allow those words to confront me and lead me forward. Like the writing of small

beetles on a tree, I am carving out my map. When the future is missing, I will reside in the letter *I*. I will abide by it, even if it topples over. Right now my

aorta is overcome with canyons. The memories carved there weigh too much in their habitual patterns. The road ahead is a bright pink dress with

hummingbirds on it. The road ahead is made of water. In this state I relearn what can be touched and not touched, by the physical body. I understand

that presence is emotional as well as corporeal. Touch is touching. I wonder what kind of molecule I am. *A fluorescent yellow oblong one.* To place the ash

of another body (even an animal's) inside your own, is a declaration of symbiosis. A denouncement of destruction. A tidal wave. A poet is also an

architect. The forms beneath the lines and the lines as constellations. The oblong body of yellow pollen alighting in blank space. We *blank* our voices

going forward into the night. Uvula as lantern. Threshold as vocal chord.

A rose is a rose is a rose. Dear Gertrude, again. She's polishing the stalactite in the sentence's caverns. Plato, dropping dead in the mud. But we start

inside the cave. Tiny Kaspar Hausers. Forgetting we have feet. Forgetting what a tongue is for. I went to the savanna to reinvent my desert page, where

grains of sand become words. Deserted. Deserved. Sand is time and so is the page. *And where is gravity?* The line. The line. The line. Poet as bacterium, or

microcosm. An insect. Slime.

The silent poetry auction begins at noon. Carla Harryman is my bodyguard. Françoise Hardy, my harlot. Have you heard of the drag queen, Jinkx

Monsoon? People say we are the same anachronism. *Soleil, je vous aime.* Soleil, when the bull charges the red. Red, red girl in the woods. She is going

to her grandmother's house where she will be consumed by a sexual predator in grandma's clothing. The first moment of spring is a chrysalis, a

preparatory or transitional state. Loose in the soil. Soleil! For Rodrigo Toscano. For the loose thread tangling in my mouth. Thrum. Thrum.

Thrum. The mountains sing. The white blood cells are charging the lineage. The white blood cells are turning against themselves. Survival has become

singular. In the lungs, or gills of fish. In the genome. A rose is a rose is an explosion. All the red dust flying in the air. That red, cellular energy.

But what we see in the light is the past.

The first sentence of the book is a woman clearing her throat. The first hypothesis, a noose. In the past life of the thread, it was a diving bell.

A hemisphere. A hemoglobin. I empty the small lake of my mouth into a test tube. This pattern will tell me where I am from by tracing the inner map

of my microbial landscape. I will learn if the family stories are true. Did my great-grandmother actually sing Otoe songs to my father in Wheaton,

Illinois, in the 1950s? Did my grandfather's Russian or Yugoslavian father receive an Anglophone revision of his name when he came to America,

before abandoning his son? Is it true that my name also is Mudd? That it was my ancestor who mended the leg of the man who shot President

Lincoln. Am I a proper villain of the Roman Empire, or the bodily echo of a series of brutalities and rape? Most likely I am half of these things and

none of them. What do I know of the depths of the lake? Except to say, *Here, look. Slain wolves exit the corner of my mouth and I am one.*

ACKNOWLEDGMENTS

Thank you to *The Elephants* for publishing a version of "Dear Andrea [I Speak in Tongues]," to my stepmother, Ágnes Giron (nee Herczeg), for her help with the Hungarian sections of this work, to Jinkx Monsoon for their vaudevillian light in the midst of this grief, and to Eric Baus, Bin Ramke, Olivia Cronk, Amy Reed, Julie Reid, Jennifer Bell, J. Michael Martinez, Teresa Veramendi, Mathias Svalina, Brian Foley, Tina Brown Celona, Carolina Ebeid, Jeffrey Pethybridge, Patrick Pethybridge, and Khadijah Queen for their friendship and their kindness.

Andrea Rexilius is the author of *The Way the Language Was* (Letter Machine, forthcoming in Spring 2020), *New Organism: Essais* (Letter Machine, 2014), *Half of What They Carried Flew Away* (Letter Machine, 2012), and *To Be Human Is To Be a Conversation* (Rescue Press, 2011). She is Core Faculty in Poetry, and Program Coordinator, for the Mile-High MFA in Creative Writing at Regis University. She also teaches in the Poetry Collective at the Lighthouse Writers Workshop in Denver, Colorado.

SIDEBROW BOOKS | www.sidebrow.net

ON WONDERLAND & WASTE

Sandy Florian

Collages by Alexis Anne Mackenzie

SB002 | ISBN: 0-9814975-1-9

BEYOND THIS POINT ARE MONSTERS

Roxanne Carter

SB009 | ISBN: 0-9814975-8-6

SELENOGRAPHY

Joshua Marie Wilkinson

Polaroids by Tim Rutili

SB003 | ISBN: 0-9814975-2-7

THE COURIER'S ARCHIVE & HYMNAL

Joshua Marie Wilkinson

SB010 | ISBN: 0-9814975-9-4

NONE OF THIS IS REAL

Miranda Mellis

SB005 | ISBN: 0-9814975-4-3

FOR ANOTHER WRITING BACK

Elaine Bleakney

SB011 | ISBN: 1-940090-00-8

LETTERS TO KELLY CLARKSON

Julia Bloch

SB007 | ISBN: 0-9814975-6-X

THE VOLTA BOOK OF POETS

A constellation of the most innovative poetry evolving today, featuring 50 poets of disparate backgrounds and traditions

SB012 | ISBN: 1-940090-01-6

SPED

Teresa K. Miller

SB008 | ISBN: 0-9814975-7-8

IN AN I

Popahna Brandes

SB013 | ISBN: 1-940090-02-4

VALLEY FEVER

Julia Bloch

SB014 | ISBN: 1-940090-03-2

H & G

Anna Maria Hong

SB019 | ISBN: 1-940090-08-3

THE YESTERDAY PROJECT

Ben Doller & Sandra Doller

SB015 | ISBN: 1-940090-04-0

THE END

MC Hyland

SB021 | ISBN: 1-940090-10-5

THE WINE-DARK SEA

Mathias Svalina

SB016 | ISBN: 1-940090-05-9

FIELD GLASS

Joanna Howard & Joanna Ruocco

SB017 | ISBN: 1-940090-06-7

INHERIT

Ginger Ko

SB018 | ISBN: 1-940090-07-5